LETTING
GO

A MOTHER'S HEALING JOURNEY
THROUGH JOURNALS, POETRY & SONG

CLAIRE MARIE
BARTON

Claire Marie Barton

Murray & McCarthy
West Cork, Ireland

This is the first printing of
"Letting Go"
– A Mother's Healing Journey –
by Claire Marie Barton

ISBN: 978-0-9556985-8-3

Published by
Murray & McCarthy Publishing
Ardfield, Clonakilty, Co. Cork
www.mcpublishing.ie

Recordings for the Audio CD were produced by Ronan Murray
in Ardfield, Clonakilty, Co. Cork
www.mcpublishing.ie

Please get in touch via my website.
I would love to hear from you.
You can also order copies of 'Letting Go' from there.
www.clairemariebarton.com

I also have a Facebook page for the book,
if you prefer to connect there.
fb.me/clairemariebartonlettinggo

10% of the profit from the sales of 'Letting Go' will be donated to Sound4Healing
'Sound4Healing' is a charity
that has been set up by the College of Sound Healing with the aim
of promoting scientific research into the benefits of sound healing.
www.sound4healing.co.uk
www.collegeofsoundhealing.co.uk/

for Alan

'A caterpillar eats green leaves everyday.
Then the time comes where it depresses itself
into a cocoon weaved from the nourishment
of its labour transformed into wisdom.
Then of its next adventure it dreams.
It dreams of flying amongst flowers.
As it forgets its caterpillar past identity,
it transforms into the butterfly'.

George Helou

Contents

Introduction 6
MY DIARIES 9
POETRY & SONG 35

Track 01 At Every Twist and Turn 36
Track 02 Roanie 38
Track 03 Swift 39
Track 04 Sweetheart Yurt 40
Track 05 Being Marram 42
Track 06 Finding the Heart Space 44
Track 07 Fulmar on the Beach 46
Track 08 The Heart of Love 47
Track 09 Baby Mine 48
Track 10 On Loss and Abundance 50
Track 11 Caramel Swirls 52
Track 12 Wellsprings 53
Track 13 New Beginnings 54
Track 14 Memorial 56
Track 15 Decade 57
Track 16 Song for Alan 58
Track 17 Interview with Alan Under the Apple Tree ... 59
Track 18 Dream Sequence 60
Track 19 Letting Go 62
Track 20 Sometime Soon 63
Track 21 Camino 64
Track 22 Tell Mama 66
Track 23 Grandmother 67
Track 24 Leanbh Na Spéire 68
Track 25 Connections 70
Track 26 Bestowed Upon Me 71
Track 27 Summer 72
Track 28 Shine 73
Track 29 Shores of Yours 74

Afterword 75
Acknowledgements 76

Introduction

For a long time now, I've wanted to write a book about my experience of my son Alan, my first-born, who died at birth on January 10, 2005. The experience made a big impact on me and I wanted to record both the sadness and the blessings of his passing. Before this could happen, I had to work on myself enough to get over my habitual fear of what others think of me and to allow myself to be vulnerable. Over the years, I have done a lot of healing energy work and this opened me up to start writing poetry and songs and begin to express myself authentically without fear.

On 1 September 2014, it was time to start my book and so I joined the Clonakilty Writer's Group. I wrote up my diaries from the time of Alan's birth but I felt too raw to share them, so over the next couple of years I brought along my poems and songs but mostly avoided writing 'the book'.

In May 2016, I completed my Angel Communication Masters course with Rev. Elvia Roe of Angels Teach University. For my course I had to do a project on anything I was passionate about. Many of my pieces were about or influenced by my experiences with Alan and when I attended a poetry workshop led by Annette Skade, she encouraged me to collate them into a chapbook, a short poetry collection on a particular theme. She showed me a couple of tribute books in memory of a loved one and that opened up the possibility of huge creative freedom for me. This was especially so in the context of having just read Elizabeth Gilbert's 'Big Magic-Creative Living Beyond Fear'. She said whenever she hears someone saying that they want to write a book because they want to help people, she says not to bother because it's too heavy. Instead she recommends you write the book for yourself in the hope that it might help you. In the process it may end up helping others.

So my angel course project started out with the aim of producing a single chapbook for myself. Photography is another passion of mine and I love taking photos as I walk in nature. This was the perfect opportunity to combine my photos and writings. Most of the pictures in this book were taken on Long Strand beach in West Cork while I listened to the recordings of my angel course classes. It is my place of inspiration for much of my writing and so this theme of rocks and sea emerged.

I would like to acknowledge and thank several of my friends: Andrea Beadle who originally encouraged me to write a book about Alan; John Riordan, who suggested adding the diary accounts to my chapbook; Afric McGlinchey who prompted me to record my songs and poems, and Ronan Murray, a local writer and publisher who, when I told him of my project, immediately offered to help me to design my book and record the pieces. I couldn't have been luckier, but in truth, this book has been guided from the very beginning. From that time in the maternity hospital when I woke in the middle of the night, with 'At every twist and turn in our lives…' going round and around inside my head until I took up my pen and started writing.

I started this book with the intention of celebrating Alan's short time on this earth, but as the project developed I realized that I was writing about my own journey and how Alan has influenced it. It didn't make sense to stop at 2005, so I reached into my diaries of the last 11 years, looking at my life and how Alan has coloured it. This has become our story.

When I was going through my diaries I found an entry in February 2015. It was where I had written a piece as part of a group exercise with Rev. Elvia. My concern at the time was the development of this book and what it was going to be. Rev. Elvia led us to imagine our loved one giving us an old-fashioned brown suitcase with pictures on it. I imagined Alan as a cherub handing it to me. When I opened it, it was full of handwritten notebooks in my writing. "Don't worry," he said, "I'm just giving it to you. It's all there. It's easy".

At the time, I didn't understand what he meant, but in the last few months it has become clear since this whole book has come from the writings in my diaries. It was there all along…

Alan has changed my life and has been such an amazing source of love, inspiration and learning. I am deeply grateful for the experience and for all the blessings he has brought me. I am delighted to be able to share this part of our journey with you.

Love & Blessings,
Claire Marie Barton
22 November, 2016

7

In the end, they brought Alan back to me in
theatre and I was able to hold him.
He never moved or opened his eyes,

My Diaries

While out on the hills recently looking for nesting hen harriers, I listened to an interview on the radio with a German lady who had adopted a 2-year-old boy. She said "The first day we just had him for a couple of hours so he could get used to us. The second day was a bit longer and to be honest I could have easily handed him back. But the third day, that was it, he became part of us and I couldn't imagine life without him". When asked was it like unconditional love that she felt, she answered "Oh no, it was much worse than that! He was wrapped around my heart muscle and was part of me". I could feel that same fierce love for Alan.

I've been in the Rotunda Hospital in Dublin for the last three hours. Tomorrow, Dr. Michael Darling will operate and hopefully remove the septum in my womb. I have a rare condition called a bicornuate uterus, which means that my womb is divided into two compartments. It should be possible to remove the septum but until he looks at it, he won't know for sure if there are going to be complications. I feel very positive generally, but at the back of my mind, I still feel like it's not over yet. There's a chance I won't be able to have any more kids. I've brought my rosary beads and my angel pictures. I feel as if I might have to be strong. I do feel strong now and whatever happens, I'm glad that we are able to bring things forward.

Last week I got upset because in theory with the op going well, I could be pregnant again soon. Then I felt very sad because it's Alan I want and having the op won't bring him back. In some ways it's all happening very quickly. Alan would be just 6 weeks old now if he was born full term. He was due on my birthday, the 7th of April 2005.

I was looking forward to an opportunity of an evening alone to write down what happened in January. It was such a special time; I don't want to forget any of the details. I'll start at the beginning.

On the 2nd of July 2004 we went to a friend's wedding in Adare. I believe Alan was conceived that night. We had a wonderful time at the wedding and had great fun dancing with all our friends and their kids. That night we both knew we were ready to have children, although we had never discussed it before other than agreeing that one day we would like to start a family.

After a month I had an unusual period, which lasted for nearly 30 days. Not knowing you could bleed during pregnancy, I assumed nothing was stirring. I thought the best thing was to wait another month and maybe I'd have some news. Sometimes I felt a bit strange and I thought I might be pregnant but assumed I couldn't be.

I was very tired and couldn't concentrate at work. In August I got very little done. The main problem was I had no conscience. Normally if I do very little work one day, I feel guilty and try to make up for it the next. At the time though, there was no guilt, I just couldn't care less really! In October, the week before the Cork Jazz Festival, I decided to take a pregnancy test.

We were on our way to Wicklow to do some fieldwork and were planning to stay with a friend. We got to Wicklow early so I nipped into the 'Grand Hotel' and did the test. While waiting the required three minutes, I read the instructions. It seemed straightforward and I took a casual look at the tester. Zap I was pregnant! I couldn't believe it and spent another good 5 minutes before I was convinced and threw away the evidence. Col guessed when he saw me haring across the car park. I had no idea how long but figured it was either a month or 3 months.

When we got home the next night we told Mum and Dad. They were thrilled but Dad thought it best to wait until I saw the doctor the following day for a re-test before he could really believe the good news. I visited the doctor the next morning and she re-tested me. From what I told her she was fairly sure I wasn't very long pregnant. She gave us a booklet about pregnancy and wanted to know what hospital we were going to and if I had been taking my folic acid. Turns out you should take the stuff 3-5 months before you get pregnant. Also it had little suggestions for taking the test like having Daddy involved too and getting him to read out the result-oops!

We decided on St Finbarr's hospital because everyone was very friendly and my brother's friend Emer was a midwife there. Our consultant was a gentle African with a good sense of humour. When he did the first examination, he said 'Sure you're nearly half-ways there!' and the scan revealed the baby to be 16 weeks old! I couldn't believe it.

We saw him kicking and moving around. It was amazing. At the time I was convinced we were going to have a girl (Sorry Alan!)- although Mum knew better and insisted it was going to be a boy all through the pregnancy. We had to skip ahead in the pregnancy book as we thought we were still at the 'paper clip' stage whereas the baby was now supposed to be the size of an avocado.

Everything was great. I was a bit worried about the bleeding I'd had and the fact that I had been drinking a few times but the doctor put my mind at rest. It explained a few things; like why I was the slowest walking up the hills on the Isle of Rum and I'd found it so tiring. Not to mind the day I was up the big ladder painting over the patio doors and big kitchen windows and calling myself a wimp for being exhausted and feeling dizzy.

I hadn't been sick and baby seemed fine so I was thrilled. I started giving him Reiki, and at night as he grew I felt him nestle in under my right hand as if to soak it up. I was amazed at how fantastic being pregnant was. Until then, I had never given it any thought other than thinking it must be uncomfortable being huge. Instead it was a beautiful experience having this little person growing inside of you, completely nurtured by you.

There were no problems until I danced too much at a Christmas party. I had felt full of energy and danced until 4.30am. Next day I felt very sore and tender and had some spotting. I was really worried and felt so guilty. I went to see the consultant and he said everything was fine and asked what kind of dancing I was up to. I stopped worrying when I saw the ultrasound and saw the baby was still moving. He gave us a fright first though because we couldn't see movement for ages and thought he was asleep or worse.

Just before Christmas, we flew to Aberdeen where we used to live, for the 'Seabirds at Sea Teams' Christmas party. I had bleeding again that week and not much movement from the baby so again became very worried. I phoned the hospital and they said not to worry. I had stopped sleeping on my back because it is supposed to be dangerous for a baby, maybe cutting off the blood supply. It was a bit more difficult to give Reiki at night. I was still worried and feeling less connected to him. On Sunday night after we got back from Aberdeen, we gave the baby the 'Elvis Crespo' treatment. We turned up the CD full blast and danced to 'Suavemente'. We decided if we got no movement, then we were in trouble. But what baby could resist and I felt movement. I think that was when Col felt his one and only kick. Relieved, I reverted to sleeping on my back again and giving Reiki and the baby moved normally again.

My other worry was that I was not really getting any bigger. I had put on no weight and my bump although visible did not seem to be growing. I was worried that my appetite was less than normal and I was trying to eat a bit more. A friend in Aberdeen who was also pregnant was way bigger although she was only due a month before me. No-one listened to me at the hospital I think because they are afraid of women becoming obsessed with their weight and dieting during pregnancy so I was not routinely weighed. My weight remained constant throughout the pregnancy.

Over Christmas, there was still worry at the back of my mind even though I knew the baby was still alive. On Stephen's Day out of the blue, I decided that I must visit the family graves and Col came with me. I prayed at each grave and asked everyone to look after my baby. In St. Oliver's graveyard on the way out, a gravestone caught my eye. It was a baby's grave entitled 'To our darling little angel'. I got a rush of emotion to my throat and felt tears in my eyes. I didn't know why then.

After Christmas, I felt optimistic. I stopped worrying and got on with it. On Saturday 8th January 2005, we went out for a meal with Mum and Dad and my brother Dave to Ma Fitz's over Macroom way. We had a lovely evening. At 11.30 pm we were back at their house watching TV when I felt a sudden rush of blood so I went to the toilet and lots of blood gushed out. I started shaking with fear. I knew it was serious. Then I pulled myself together and went out and told Col we had to go to the hospital.

My consultant wasn't there but luckily another consultant, Dr Greene, was in the hospital as he was performing a caesarean. A few other nurses and doctors tried unsuccessfully to find the heartbeat. Dr Greene eventually came in and found it straight away. It was erratic. He did a scan and wasn't happy. The baby was much too small. They might have to do an emergency section or maybe I'd have to lie down for the next few months and see if that would improve things. We wouldn't know until Monday when we'd get a detailed scan. A beautiful young doctor who looked like Sade took blood samples and gave me steroid injections in my thighs. This is to boost the lung capacity of premature babies. I didn't feel any pain. I was numb to it and just cried for my baby.

I shared a room with a Chinese Malaysian girl. She had a miscarriage at 11 weeks. She works in a Chinese restaurant every day till 1.30 am. Twelve hour shifts standing, preparing veggies. She was meant to be going home soon to have the baby. Now she wouldn't be going. She didn't have much English. "Baby gone". With the curtain drawn between us, we both cried ourselves to sleep.

Next day she left and a woman in labour arrived. It was her first. She was in pain. My mind was racing with possibilities and what if's. One of the midwives advised me to take it one day at a time, and not to worry. She said 'At the moment, you still have a baby, concentrate on what is and deal with anything else as it happens'. I took her advice and felt better.

On Monday morning (10 January), I had a detailed scan. I recognised the sonographer from Bishopstown. She was very good. She confirmed that the baby was around 500g and should have been double that and that the placenta was poorly developed. Physically the baby seemed okay but difficult to know really. The heartbeat was erratic because the blood supply to the baby was irregular. They would need to operate sooner rather than later.

After lunch I was moved to the Erinville hospital by taxi. They have better facilities there for premature babies. It was a bit freaky because I already knew this and about the steroid injections, because a friend of mine had been through this recently. I was put fasting immediately and had another scan.

In the evening, I was brought up to theatre. Everyone was lovely and the anaesthetist was fantastic. He explained what was going to happen. I got a spinal epidural and my legs went dead. It didn't really hurt at all. They put a 'tent' over me so I couldn't see the op. I had the sensation of cutting, then the doctor rooting around. It felt really weird so I asked Col to keep talking to me. We chatted away, discussed going to Darwin on our holidays to see my sister Lou. We put on a brave front-laughing and joking. All that day I felt immensely calm and peaceful. I had no worries. I felt it was the Reiki Lou was sending from Australia.

At 19.43 Alan was born. I was 27 weeks pregnant. He was so tiny, so beautiful, I cried. He was whisked away immediately to the special baby unit by a lovely man, Dr. Ali. It took a while to stitch me up. Dr. Ali came back after 5 minutes and said that Alan was only 375 g. He was too small to survive and he couldn't keep him much longer. I sent Col off to see him, in case he died before I got out of theatre. Col came back crying because he thought I wouldn't get to see him. I thought Dr. Greene would never finish. As well as finding a septum in my womb, he also found I had endometriosis around my left ovary so he cut that out.

In the end, they brought Alan back to me in theatre and I was able to hold him. He never moved or opened his eyes. It was hard to tell if he was alive or dead but it was clear he didn't have long. We were brought into the recovery room by a very nice nurse and left alone with Alan. Col went and phoned Mum and Dad and they came in with my brother Dave. Mum's camera wasn't working very well and the nurse let us use the hospital Polaroid. It wasn't great because Alan was so small and the camera couldn't focus up close. Still it is the only photo we have of the three of us and it is really precious to have.

We were asked if we had any names chosen. We had only one in mind and that was Alan. It felt right so we decided he would be Alan and not nameless 'Baby Barton'. The nurse made a remembrance booklet for us with handprints and footprints –all so tiny. She even cut a tiny lock of hair, which wasn't easy because it was so fine and silky and short.

Dad suggested calling a priest but I said it was too late that he was dead. After an hour or so another nurse came in and looked for a pulse and officially declared him dead. It was all very unreal. I was still numb from the anaesthetic and had to lie flat on my back. We were all crying but amazed at the little miracle in our midst. The first grandchild in our family.

Col was allowed to stay the night because of what happened. They brought Alan to us and put him in a cot nearby. As far as I can remember, we didn't hold him. We were both exhausted and felt there was no point. It was too late. After a while they took him away as he had to be put in the morgue.

The next day, reality was beginning to set in and there were many tears. The staff were fantastic and I was allocated two midwives: Annette for the night shift and Ciara during the day. They both encouraged me to spend some time with Alan saying they'd bring him up to me any time I wanted. They said it was very therapeutic for most women and they couldn't recommend it enough. At first I thought it was a bit strange but that evening after everyone had gone home, I asked for Alan to be brought to me. It was such a relief to see him again and to hold him. When he was there I felt I could connect to him spiritually and that he was there with me.

From the start, I felt very much like there had been no mistake and that everything had happened as it was meant to. Alan had chosen to come for a very short time and although we found it very sad, that was how it was meant to be. At that stage we didn't know what the implications were regarding my womb and I was very aware that I might not be able to have any other children. And yet having had Alan and becoming parents was a fantastic experience that neither of us would have missed out on for anything.

That night going to sleep I felt Alan was still there in the room and there were many others too. It felt crowded but very peaceful and joyful. I slept very well and at one stage I woke and felt like I was lifted off the bed and lovingly cradled and supported.

The next day I got a loan of our friend Mark's digital camera and that night I took several pictures of Alan, knowing it would be my last chance, to get a proper record of what he looked like. Today I am delighted to have these photos. It takes a while to learn a face and if I didn't have them I wouldn't have a clear picture in my head of Alan and that's very important to me. That night I also did a couple of drawings as a way to express and record my love and my emotions at the time. I had been impressed by the art in Pam England's 'Birthing from Within' book and felt it would be a good way of expressing my grief. I also wanted to write something profound that would summarise the whole experience of having Alan. I had always intended writing this diary but I was afraid I would be too clinical and just describe what happened and at what time and just miss out on the essence of it all. I wasn't sure what to write though so I said I'd leave it till the morning. I was still very stiff and sore and couldn't move very much except occasionally to struggle out to the toilet. This I could just about do without fainting. I was propped up in bed with pillows and had a small light on overhead all the time.

I went off to sleep. In the middle of the night, I woke with "At every twist and turn in our lives" repeating itself in my head over and over. At first I tried to ignore it but then I began to think maybe I should write it down and it would be the start of something. I reached out for my diary and put it on my chest and started to write. At the angle I was at, I couldn't really see what I was doing. I tried to keep my mind blank and just write whatever came. I wrote in spurts. There'd be a pause, and then more would come. It was very strange as I had no idea what was going to come out and I didn't pay any attention to it at the time, I just let it keep coming. Eventually I felt I was finished and I closed the book and went back to sleep again. I wasn't sure who had actually written it whether it was my soul or Alan or angels-I still don't know really.

The next morning I asked Mum to come to me, and I showed her and Ciara my drawings and we all had tears. It felt very special showing them and just talking. I waited for Col to come to see me and we read the piece I'd written together. I really didn't remember most of it. Col was amazed.

Two chaplains at the Mercy Hospital came to visit during the week; Fr Humphrey and Fr. Michael O'Regan. Both were very kind and added another dimension to the wonderful people we met that week. We had been thinking of ways we could celebrate Alan and Fr Humphrey suggested planting a tree. He has a tree in his garden for each of his nephews and nieces. It was one of the things we had been thinking of and Col wanted us to plant a willow, which would be perfect. It was great Fr. Michael visited too because he was one of our parish priests when I was a child so he seemed very familiar to me and we had deep spiritual conversations.

My auntie Pat and uncle Mathew were delegated to buy Alan an outfit with the instruction to buy the smallest one they could find. Ciara suggested one of the toy shops as they have dolls clothes, which are suitable for premature babies. Unfortunately the shop was closed and they spent all day scouring town, and in the end arrived with several options. I had to smile at the size of some of them- absolutely massive! Of course they hadn't actually seen Alan and didn't realise just how small he was and they had bought the smallest things they could find.

There was one lovely baby-grow with a matching hat that said 'little bundle'. Ciara took them away and dressed him up, making adjustments with sellotape to make them fit. He looked so cute!

That evening Mum and Dad and Dave and Ciara came with us to the chapel where Fr. Michael led a small intimate service for Alan. There was gentle music playing, candles lit, Ciara had made a posy of lovely flowers and Alan was dressed up and lying in his Moses basket. I had to go in a wheelchair, as I was still quite weak.

On Thursday my friends Ger and Rebecca came to visit. Up until then, I hadn't spoken to anyone outside the family because I hadn't felt ready. It must have been really hard for Col because he'd had to contact everyone and sort out work deadlines etc. I thought of this week in hospital as my time to grieve and spend time with Alan without having to talk to my friends. It was nice to see the girls when they came in. I know it was very hard for them.

I had decided not to see Alan anymore after Wednesday night, but I saw him again Thursday night because I couldn't bear not to. I'm really lucky Ciara and Annette both encouraged me to spend time with Alan as it was very important just to get to know his face and I found it much easier to connect with him spiritually when he was there in body. Forde's funeral home donated a baby coffin, which was very kind. It was only 2 foot long. We picked up Alan in his coffin on our way home on Friday morning. I felt very vulnerable leaving the cocoon of the hospital.

We put Alan in the front room in Mum and Dad's house and opened the top. Mum was very anxious about this at first but I was adamant. We lit candles including a lovely honey scented one I'd got for Mum in Lewis. For such a tiny person, he had such a powerful presence in the room and when I'd go in I'd feel deeply peaceful. Pat and Mathew came to see him for the first time and only then realised how small he was! Ger called over and it was nice to be able to show her my baby. My auntie Ann Kearney also visited.

On Saturday we headed back home with Alan. Fr. Michael had suggested that it would be a good idea to bring him home before we buried him. We put the coffin in the sitting room. A while later Mum, Dad, Dave, Pat and Mathew joined us. Dave had his new car, a Volvo Estate and he was the official hearse. As we'd been driving down from Cork, the weather was pretty miserable and it was raining. As we turned the corner into Ardfield, there was a brightness in the sky and the rain stopped. We had a simple service at the grave in Ardfield with our parish priest Fr. McCarthy.

Dad was great and had made all the funeral arrangements including organising the plot in the graveyard, and himself and Mum insisted on paying. It fits three and myself and Col will be going there too. I find that comforting. The grave digger filled in the grave while we waited as apparently this is the custom in the country when burying babies. We got a little wooden cross for the grave. Afterwards we went back to the house for tea and sandwiches and cake.

When everyone left, I was exhausted and went up to bed for a rest before we headed back to Cork. It was very surreal because the last time I had lain in that bed I was pregnant and had no idea of what was about to happen. The bed smelled of the pregnant me. I had a lovely body lotion especially for pregnant skin. It made me very sad as the extent of our loss began to sink in.

We spent the following week with Mum and Dad, which was great because I was so weak and couldn't do very much. I had visitors every night; Ger, Eleanor, Rebecca and Marjorie. Everyone was fantastic and brought lovely flowers. Padraig and Lorraine came up from West Cork too and it was great to see them. Lots of supportive texts too. When we got home the following week, there were stacks of cards from all our friends particularly from Scotland waiting for us- it was very overwhelming. All this love and support in the midst of sadness-bittersweet.

We took another few weeks before we went back to work. Not sure what we did really. The day I was leaving the hospital, the tea lady said good-bye and said, "Get him to take you somewhere nice". It seemed like a great idea and we booked a week in Lanzarote in the lovely Fariones Hotel apartments. It was a great break and beforehand it gave us something to look forward to. Towards the end of the week though we knew we'd have to return to normal life and that was hard.

September 2005

Far from being the end of a chapter in my life, Alan is still very much a part of it and he has opened new doors. This last year has been very spiritual and I feel myself opening up more although I don't always understand what's going on.

The first great thing has been an introduction to angels. This started 10 years ago actually in 1995 when I bought an angel greeting card for my sister thinking it would make a nice birthday card as she was getting into angels at the time. I put it in a safe place and totally forgot about it.

Before Christmas when Col and I were doing fieldwork up in Wicklow, we did some Christmas shopping in Wicklow town and I went into the health shop. I was taken by Lorrie's angel greeting cards that were for sale. At first I wasn't sure if they were real or not but there was a leaflet explaining how Lorraine Coffey had met her angels and began to paint them after an injury which prevented her developing her sporting career as a javelin thrower. The leaflet said she had opened an angel sanctuary in Rathdrum. I felt immediately that I would go there when Lou was next back from Australia. The cashier was very enthusiastic and said often when Lorrie came to the shop she would bring an angel and it was great. The cards felt very powerful and as we were driving back to Cork, I took them out of the dash and cried while I looked at them although I didn't know why. When we got to Bishopstown, Dad had moved the last few bits and pieces we had there, down to the end bedroom, as they were doing a spring clean. On the locker beside the bed was the angel card I had bought Lou all those years ago and it turned out to be one of Lorrie's angel cards! Dad couldn't really explain why he'd put it there, he just had.

After Christmas my friend Lorraine lent me a pack of angel cards. I kept drawing the same card. Angel of Wednesday, of Aries and of strength. The book with the cards said this was normal and it is important to listen to the message and to act on it. Not to be always looking for more messages. It's not a quick win situation if you genuinely want to learn and move forward.

When Lou came home in the summer we went to visit the angel sanctuary. We stayed in a really nice B&B in Rathdrum and had an amazing meal at the Stonecutters. Next morning we got to the Sanctuary at 10am. We were the first there and Eugene, Lorrie's husband opened up the gallery for us. While he was unlocking the door, I could sense the energy within the Sanctuary and emotion just gushed through me. He lit some candles and put on some meditation music and left us alone. I had switched my phone to silent but felt I should have switched it off completely. I didn't though and a few minutes later there was interference with the CD player as my phone was near it so I did turn it off then. I'm sure I was being asked to turn it off!

The Sanctuary is a large room painted white with a couple of alcoves and large paintings of angels all round. There were chairs and you could just sit in front of any of the pictures. I was drawn to the first picture inside the door- the angel of strength. Some pictures had messages underneath and this is what the angel of strength said " I have come to help you move forward and away from what causes you to struggle". Very similar to the angel book message. I now know this is Archangel Michael. I stayed there for a long time and cried a lot. I didn't quite know why but there was a release. I went to all the paintings, some affected me more than others especially the ones with babies in them. I guess in some ways I had come for answers about Alan even though I'm sure I already knew then at some level. After quite a lot of crying, I arrived at the Angel of Calm with her big beautiful soft pink wings. And as I looked at her, I could feel calmness flowing through me and the crying stopped. It was an amazing healing experience. When we came out, we realised we'd been in there for 3 hours. Lou enjoyed it too and could connect to the energies of the pictures. It was very profound and very healing although I can't explain what happened really.

I started reading Roz Lawlor's book 'Truth Speaks-Spirit Shares Wisdom in Humour and Light" shortly after Alan's death. It's been very helpful explaining the ways of angels and messages. In particular there are nice messages from baby angels explaining why they left so soon. I had told a friend of mine, Frances about these messages but had only sent her copies after I'd seen her in September 2005. She got them just after she'd miscarried her third baby. I didn't know she had been pregnant again.

That brings me back to what Frances told me the week after Alan died. I had seen her in August 2004 when I was newly pregnant but completely oblivious. She said when she walked in the door she knew I was pregnant. She didn't say anything. Again I met her again in October and she was positive I was pregnant but again didn't say anything and I still didn't have a clue. The weekend I went into hospital with the bleed, she was 11 weeks pregnant and felt something wasn't right. On the Sunday night she had a very vivid and significant dream about the two of us both with our bumps. On Monday she went to the hospital and was told her baby had died. That was the same day I had the emergency caesarean and Alan died. When she told me that I felt strangely comforted as again it emphasized that everything had happened as it was meant to.

When Lou told me Roz Lawlor in Australia could do a reading over the phone, I was very interested but felt it was not the right time. I asked for guidance, and on the week of Alan's first anniversary I got the go ahead. Speaking to Roz helped a lot and I gained more clarity on what had happened. She said that Alan chose us for a new beginning. He gave us enough movement for reassurance but most of the time he was out of body as he was not planning to stay long. He had no pain which was a great relief to hear. My doubts were to help prepare for the shock of his passing. She said that Frances's baby had been Alan's partner in a previous life and they had come back together. She also said he was one of my guides.

Since Alan's death, I feel him present on many occasions. Always as something small and round just beside the right side of my head. It took me a while to work out for sure if it was him but then one day it struck me that it must be him because he was confined to the right side of my womb.

For ages I was hoping he would talk to me or make contact. One night when we were staying in Bishopstown, I had my second ever lucid dream. Once I realised, I wondered what I would do? Suddenly I thought of Alan and said I want to talk to Alan. At that moment, something started to happen; I could feel bright lights and had the sensation of floating. I was going to meet Alan. I was so excited I actually woke up and that was that. I was so close…

Since Alan died I have been reading more spiritual books. I went into Waterstones shortly after looking for the right book to give me meaning and comfort. I had intended seeing if they had a section on grief. I never got there because I went straight over to a shelf and picked out a book by Deepak Chopra (who I had never heard of). It was called Synchrodestiny. That book was my new map and explained there are no such things as coincidences. One of the nice things I learnt in Synchrodestiny was 'Namaste'. This sanskrit greeting translates as 'the spirit in me acknowledges the spirit in you'. You can say this silently to people you see. I've felt a connection by doing this with an old bent-over lady I saw walking in Dublin while I was on the bus and it has also changed how I view handicapped people too, realising that whatever their difficulties, their souls are intact and perfect.

Another book I read was the autobiography of Mia Dolan, an English woman who developed her psychic gifts. She lost a baby too. I felt that the book was very significant but couldn't exactly say why. One thing that stood out was that her brother Pete died and she found it hard to let go. He said he couldn't be around all the time. I've tried not to be a bind to Alan. I wish him every happiness in his new life and just enjoy the fact that he checks in every now and again.

I believe Alan helped me to join the local Amnesty International group in Clonakilty. I had been putting off joining Amnesty since I was in my twenties. When Alan died it gave me the push to just do it. Life is too short to put important things off. My first meeting was in February 2005. I climbed the stairs in O'Donovan's Hotel and on the landing there was a sign to the left for a bereavement group and a sign to the right for the Amnesty group. I hesitated. I didn't know there was a bereavement group. Maybe I should go there. I took a deep breath and went into the Amnesty meeting. I'm so glad I did as I have made wonderful friends and it's very fulfilling. In September, I attended my first Amnesty conference and I went with my father to see Noam Chomsky speaking on the war on terror. I regularly write letters on behalf of prisoners of conscience and to various ministers in the Dail on matters ranging from women's' rights to mental health issues.

I thank Alan for that.

****

What happened next?

The operation in May was successful and a year later I gave birth to my second son Cillian. This pregnancy went fine without complications although I did worry for the first few weeks. It was an irrational fear but I was terrified of experiencing that loss again. I was driving home one evening and I came to a fork in the road. Before Alan was born I used to turn right as a short cut but after he died, I used to go left so I could drive past the graveyard instead. Because I was used to going right, every time I had to remember and I would think of Alan at that fork. So that evening I was driving and stressing about my baby when I heard a quiet voice in my head saying 'It's going to be alright'. I was distracted and hardly heard it but it was repeated clearly 3 times. Once I listened, I realised it was a message to say that this baby was going to be okay and I never worried after that.

Because of Alan's tiny size I asked for a big baby this time. I was huge in the pregnancy so there was no problem there and our second son Cillian was 10 lb 4oz, when he was born.

Three years later in 2009, we had another son Jamie. This time I asked for an eight pounder. He was 8lb leaving the hospital.

At first I never spoke about Alan to anyone who didn't already know. I thought it would be too much for them. But then a friend of mine who had also lost her baby told me how she had been in a shoe shop and told the attendant in passing about her baby and the attendant knew someone close to her who had a similar experience. This was a revelation to me, the idea of telling complete strangers in random places and they could handle it. I then realised that if I was okay about it, others would be fine too. This has been a big gift and now I am not afraid to talk to people about death and my experience of it.

When I talk to women who have had a miscarriage, they often say that of course it was much worse for me because I was farther along. To be honest I think it's much harder for them because miscarriage is not spoken about openly in Ireland. Many couples have not told anyone about their pregnancy and have to bear the grief and loss alone while pretending everything is okay and going back to work and getting on with life as normal.

Because I was 27 weeks pregnant, my baby was acknowledged and I got support which was incredibly important.

I wish we had more transparency around miscarriage and could offer the same support to all the mums and dads affected.

Speak your truth, 21 March 2011

This keeps coming up! I realised how important this was at Jo Beth Young's singing workshop. We were 'sounding' while lying on the ground and after a while my jaw started shaking from all the years when I haven't been speaking my truth and I realised the many masks I have been wearing in my life, always afraid to be myself. During that sounding these masks were starting to slip off to such an extent that I felt I had no physical face. I experienced great clarity as the real me was able to look out from inside. I felt huge relief but also the realisation of the toll it had taken. How I sacrificed my authenticity for niceness.

I have since experienced this 'no face' sensation when I feel clarity and truth and when I am in a space of really expressing my authentic self. I have to constantly practice speaking my truth because my habit is to be nice.

I had been doing a course learning about angels with Helen Harrington and at Jo Beth's workshop I started to see a connection between voice and spirituality. Over the next few years I did lots of singing workshops and in one of them I felt an angel right in front of me.

On my way to Clonakilty, I asked Alan to be there and my intention was to let go of baggage and clutter. Straight away she saw an angel down at my left foot carrying a tiny baby. During the session Pamela said there was lots of energy pouring through her hands into my head for healing. She said there was a lot of guilt there that I didn't realise I'd held onto.

Nana Riordan's birthday, 29 June 2012

Lovely IET session again with Pamela. I felt that my Nana and Grandad Riordan were with me. I think my Nana was giving me healing. I felt hands at the back of my head and energy pouring in. At first I thought it was Pamela because it felt so physical but then she started talking and I realised she was down near my feet. She left us on our own for a few minutes and it was lovely. Later my Dad texted to say it was Nana Riordan's birthday and she would have been 101 today. So that was my confirmation!

Women's Christmas, 6 January 2015

Alan's Anniversary is coming up on Saturday . I want to write something to celebrate him and to show my gratitude for all the gifts he has given me. Last year I found his birthday hard. This year too around Christmas I found myself having moments of grieving in the car, suddenly erupting when I've been on my own driving into Clon and again when driving to Cork for Christmas when the others had gone ahead. Since I started opening up to myself with the energy work with Maan Kantar in 2013, I'm allowing myself to feel my emotions. This can be very intense and yet it assures me I am alive and present. When I was pregnant with Jamie, I went to osteopath Natalie Rousseau for treatments as I had a lot of sciatica during the pregnancy. I had a treatment coming up to 27 weeks of pregnancy and I felt lots of sadness and fear even though I fully believed all was well with this baby. She explained that my body was remembering the pain and the loss that came at 27 weeks previously. She helped me to express the pain and sorrow that my body felt deeply. Then she asked me how I felt. I said 'My sadness feels safe'. While I want to heal fully from my loss, I never want to take away from the experience by forgetting or not feeling anymore. So for me it is important to acknowledge my sadness when it comes up. For me Alan is both the saddest and most beautiful experience of my life. He has been the key to my awakening, to my desire to live life to the full, to explore my purpose in life and to start living the life I want to lead. Ten years on, this keeps unfolding and I know he is by my side supporting me whenever I need him. I am so grateful for the many gifts he has given me- the gift of becoming a mother, first to him and then by highlighting the problem in my womb, I was able to have the operation to remove the septum allowing me to have 2 healthy boys. Alan helped me tune into my intuition so I could feel his presence and now a growing awareness of angels and all they do to help us in our daily lives.

Alan's 10th Anniversary, 10 January, 2015

My intention today is to connect with Alan. Today on the way back from the graveyard, I was thinking about Alan and wondering if he would give me a sign and then I saw a rainbow in the direction of the graveyard and felt it was a message from him. Later I did an angel card reading for myself and picked a card showing a family of four waving up at a rainbow. Today this card felt like our little family waving to our loved one in the sky who made the rainbow.

Message from the Sea, 15 April 2015

Sometimes things that don't come our way,
can come back another day
(when we let go of attachment).

I found the missing pen!
Waiting for me, loosely wrapped
in a curl of seaweed strand-
presented on sparkling sand.

At first I hoped that was all I'd find-
that one missing pen that drifted out of my grasp,
teased me a few times then headed out to sea.
I felt the powerful gift of the pen
that sea gave to me.
Today it felt very clear.

The other day when I found 18 pens on the beach,
I laughed when Col said maybe it was a sign I was supposed to write!
I laughed because for starters, I'm the hippy around here
and he doesn't believe in signs,
and then because I hadn't actually understood the message although it couldn't have
been more blatant!
But today I understood the significance and generosity of the gift.
There are no limitations- you can write.

When I found the new pen, I was thankful but felt that if I did find more then it
wouldn't be quite so special. In minutes I found 5 more along a short stretch of beach.
Then I realised I had been limiting myself, closing myself off to the abundance that was
there for me. So I said thanks again and picked them all up and as I walked, I felt so
abundant and yet I knew that there was the possibility of more and I felt myself open to
it, not in a greedy or needy way- just knowing it as a possibility.

In the magical land of the strand,
there is time for tea
and time for me.

7 September 2014

Okay I get it.
It is not about me anymore.
By talking openly about Alan,
I give others permission to do the same.
I shine my light on their loss
and that's where the healing can begin.

A young pied wagtail just landed on the roof and looked in at me.
I remember asking for a gift from my angels before, and a pied wagtail came to the
same spot as I sat there looking out.
He stayed for several minutes eyeing me intently- connecting.
Today's wagtail is a reminder of that day- the gift.

28

Today's wagtail is young and eager to learn.
He is getting his bearings,
just learning to fly
as am I.

"Respect the time needed to develop maturity and knowing.
This process does not have to be rushed.
You just have to fly everyday,
and the wind will take you to where
you need to be
if you let her,
Trust and glide
with an open excited heart.
Feel the connection with all,
now and always."

I am aware that Grace has been ever-present this week. Just the way it was the week after Alan was born. Everything flowed and had a sense of purpose and significance. Nuggets and gems in every conversation or experience, to be acted on, or digested at a later stage. There was an openness in me. I surrendered to life. I asked for help and help flooded in cloaked in Grace. I had never understood that song-'Amazing Grace' I didn't know what it meant. Now I can feel grace, a tangible blessing in my life, uplifting me when I need it and least expect it. And when in a state of grace I am carried along, my feet hardly touch the ground, not feeling any bumps on the road, for there is a magnificent simplicity which arrives. A humility that allows a being in the moment and a highlighted awareness of all the natural beauty in our world, that is there all the time waiting for us to notice. Carrying golden keys in dew-tangled webs-ready to unlock our own cramped hearts.

Our hearts need space to grow, to expand because LOVE should not be boxed in. It wants to be seen. It wants to look, explore, admire, encourage, empathise, affirm, support, hold, comfort, empower. It wants to go far and expand our world, bursting all illusion en route. It wants to add colour in our lives-the magnificence of the rainbow bathing us in shimmering light. It wants to wash away our worries, our fears, our great fears of the known and the unknown. It wants to tell us about the sun, about happiness, about hope, about the joy of being. It wants to tell us about source and our connection to it. Yes, that we are connected to source at all times and have divine light, of the pure light sparks that we are. And all we are asked to do is to open the window of our hearts and let the LOVE flow.

I remember Auntie Joan telling me that she had to move over in the bed for Uncle George (and that was after he died). Such beautiful devotion and love that transcends death and we have nothing to fear. For stretching out to the end of time, there is only LOVE.

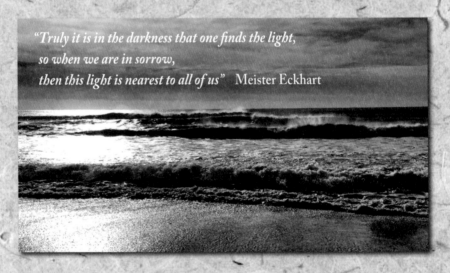

"Truly it is in the darkness that one finds the light, so when we are in sorrow, then this light is nearest to all of us" Meister Eckhart

Angel Communication exercise, 10 November, 2014

Close your eyes and take 3 deep breaths.
Now open your eyes.

What do you see?
The back of the chair- the 3 pieces of wood together in the middle.

What do you hear?
The rain on the window

What do you feel?
Shock, expectancy, a readiness, a calling to do something, a bit anxious

What do you know?
That there is significance in the number 3. That there are 3 elements involved-they are equal and interlinked. Resolution depends on the 3 aspects being acknowledged and dealt with.

The symmetry is also important. I'm reminded of the rhythm John Bowker showed us yesterday on the bells, it's the same forwards and backwards-palindrome.

Three in numerology refers to expression.

The symmetry shows a divine plan on the way to ultimate self-expression. There are 3 strands, all inextricably linked. First self-expression through poetry and song, then the book about Alan and then integrating these truths into all aspects of my life.

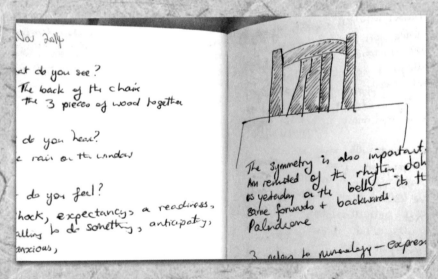

Once you become 'REAL', it cannot be undone.

The rain symbolises the challenges and self-doubt but it isn't even that heavy and in fact I am safe and warm and dry inside. I do not need to worry about the rain. In fact it's stopped now.

I can start with any or all strands. They all feed each other. Nothing is happening in isolation. The results are solid teak-definitely real. This is not self-absorption, this is actually very solid. Fears about being wishy-washy are just self-doubt and it is time to move into self-trust.

29 December 2015

Dear Alan, have you any message for me at this moment?
'My dearest Mama, I am always with you and I love you. The book will be fine, don't worry. Just go and do it and I will be there in the background.'

Do you want to write anything in it?
'I already have and in truth my essence is already in the pages.'

11 January 2016

It was Alan's birthday yesterday. He would have been 11. I went to mass with the boys and Fr. McCarthy called out his Anniversary. We lit a candle for him after and I thanked Alan for all the gifts he has given me.

At home Jamie made up an altar with Alan's things and he did a lovely job. Cillian read some of the cards and letters, in our 'Memories of Alan Box. He read aloud a letter my friend Winnie from Zambia had written and it sounded so poignant in his clear child's voice. I think we were all feeling a bit sad so I suggested we pick some angel cards to see what messages Alan had for us. Col picked 'Think happy thoughts!'
We made banana chocolate muffins and after lunch headed up to the graveyard. We had our traditional picnic of hot chocolate and muffins at the picnic area beside the graveyard, leaving a muffin of course for Alan. This always sparks the question as to who might eat it…
We played a couple of games of tennis before heading home.

****

Artwork by Cillian Barton

My heart has opened
and I feel the pain inside.
I allow it just to be

Poetry & Song

At Every Twist and Turn

At every twist and turn in our lives
we are faced with uncertainty.
As experiences unfold, we don't know
which direction they will take.
All that we can do is yield to the events
and see where it takes us in life,
to new levels of awareness.
Enrichment and love come along the way
sometimes forged through a path of pain.
We cannot have one without the other.
Everything is connected and linked.
There are no coincidences.
We can be surer of the way if we listen to the small voice,
often in the background, mouthing unseen.
If we listen to that voice of truth and intuition,
we stand to learn so much.

Over Christmas, I visited the graveyards to connect
with Nan and Grandad Poll, Auntie Minnie, Nana & Grandad Riordan,
Kevin, Evelyn, and Mrs. O'Sullivan.
I asked them all for help with my baby.
I didn't realise he would be meeting them so soon.
I remember the grave of "Our Little Angel"-
it stirred emotions in me,
made me think of my own little angel that I would soon have to give up.
Our little angel was on loan- just for a very short time he was in our lives.
Even so, he has changed us.

We now have a son.
We have experienced the tender love that a parent feels for their child.
Our son is beloved. He has left us with memories,
the tiniest little boy ever-so small and perfect, so serene and peaceful.
His short life has held no strife.
He survived in the dark softness of my womb,
sometimes feeling a hand of Reiki and nestling into my palm.

Trusting innocent, unself-conscious babe.
Little exploratory tumbles and turns in his own secret den.
Happy to hear Daddy asking about his bambino in his gentle curious way.
Touching my stomach looking for clues to his beautiful son within.
Gently massaging just saying hello, our son learns about his Daddy.
A patient son who politely listens while his mum tries to learn the clarinet,
or decides that it's time he was introduced to Elvis Crespo.
Thank-you Alan for choosing us to be your parents.
And yet already, it is you who is now nurturing us.
We will keep you always in our hearts.
Your resting place in Ardfield will be ours too one day.
Maybe it will be soon- maybe many years from now. Love is timeless.
Love keeps us together always. We will always be together.
I hope you like your new sea view in Ardfield.

My lovely bump has disappeared.
I have full breasts waiting for a babe to feed.
Alan we miss you but we know you had to go.
The small voice has told me in the past
that one day there would be sadness and suffering.
Now it is here, I realise it is bittersweet.
Love, loss, sadness and peace all inextricably bound.

We take the package, the present that was you,
entrusted to our care by the Divine.
We accept the outcome. We learn to be gracious. We have learnt
much and yet we have not fully unravelled the present
or it's significance in the future. We have to wait and be guided.

Little bambino,
little blue hat, little bundle.
Daddy's blond hair.
Nana's hands.
Daddy's toes.
Mammy's chin.
Little bambino where are you?'

Roanie

It felt as though Roanie and her kittens were sent to us on loan to help us through the numbness after Alan was gone.

They thought she was ours,
we thought she was theirs.
Lived alone in the hedge,
a small bundle of fur.

When he discovered the truth,
Dad fed her.
Cautiously
won her over.

Later realising
her full belly was not from his care,
he made a nest
in the shed behind the lawn mower.

Cats never seem to use the bed you make them
but Roanie gave birth there
in safety behind bicycle wheels,
in the grass collector, lined with old woollen jumpers.

Three kittens.
Maxi the boy
and two sisters
Spikey and Stripey.

We poured our love
that we had been saving
into these furry bodies.

My mother doesn't do cats but Maxi Pussy thrived
in her arms and was allowed on her sofas.
The girls came to live with us in the country.
Eased our loneliness.

When another baby filled my womb,
they would sit on my bump, purring.
But when he was six months old, all the cats had gone,
their job done.

Swift

This is the first song I wrote. It was in 2013 during a songwriting workshop with Caz Jeffries. It started out just noticing the sparrows and the swifts that were outside but then quickly went to my pain and longing to soar high in the sky and leave everything behind.

Oh to be a Swift on the wing,
for weeks and weeks.
Skimming the water for a bath.
Manic chases
down the narrow streets,
on a trip to the town.

Later, flying over mountains
looking down,
I see ribbons of rivers.
It's so quiet up here,
far, far far from the sparrows
that are chirping.

Oh to be a Swift on the wing,
for weeks and weeks.
I remember flying and dancing,
at the same time doing somersaults.

I am free,
flying higher and higher
into the sky.
It is turquoise,
I am feeling light.
I fly over the mountains
looking down,
on the rivers like ribbons.
It's so quiet up here.

Should I go back?
I long, I long to stay right here,
for a while,

for a while.
I feel light.

Oh to be a Swift on the wing,
for weeks and weeks.
Skimming the water for a bath.
Manic chases
on the narrow streets,
on a trip to town.

Later flying over mountains
looking down,
I see ribbons of rivers.
It's so quiet up here,
far, far far from the sparrows,
that are chirping.

I am free, free;
flying higher and higher in the sky,
I am free;
flying higher and higher in the sky,
I am free.
flying higher and higher in the sky,
I am free.

39

Sweetheart Yurt

To celebrate our 10th wedding anniversary, Col and I went away for a weekend to Scotland to see Belle & Sebastian in concert in Inverness. It was the first time in the seven years since Cillian and Jamie were born that we had been away on our own. We stayed in a yurt in Glen Nevis and this song is about our love, being in a beautiful place and feeling the sentience of mountains.

Gentle rain idles the roof.
Canvas accepts, patiently listening to it's story.
It's been told many, many times before.

Inside all is peaceful.
Candles and lanterns stand sentry round the edges,
emphasizing the circular form of the yurt.

The stove crackles contentedly,
the air is warm and smells of wood smoke.
The red-painted slats circle overhead,
adorned with colourful flowers.

A midnight snack, bread sticks and hummus.
It's late, Astrud serenades us gently.
It's time for sleep, we travel tomorrow,
back to the beautiful west Cork and our blue-eyed boys.

This time we have to reconnect,
watched over by imposing mountains, unfazed by man or beast.
They've seen it all before yet they do not judge.

They are just there for us, helping us with
pieces of the puzzle that is our lives.
Offering opportunities for contemplation;
of silence and of going within.
Forming a back-drop to our re-connection with our inner world,
which we often times don't see.

These mountains bear witness to us,
at times a hard task master, pushing us further, higher and higher.
Focussing our minds completely on our breath
and the next step we will take.

Relentlessly, higher and higher and higher,
until there is nothing in our minds but the present moment.
These gifts from these mighty giants who ask for
nothing in return, except for peace.

Gentle rain idles the roof.
Canvas accepts, patiently listening to it's story,
It's been told many, many times before.

Sweetheart yurt, Glen Nevis today.
Sweetheart yurt, Glen Nevis today.
Sweetheart yurt, Glen Nevis today.

Being Marram

I love Long Strand. It has been my refuge over the years. Its not so much walking it I love as finding a place to sit down to write or just be. One glorious day in November when I was being, I became marram.

Brilliant sunshine warms,
and we have come out en masse to embrace it.
The sea ripples azure.
Clean waves break
precisely.
White horses with back-lit manes
race for shore.

Cocooned from the wind,
I sit on sand
drinking sunlight
and the sounds of the sea;
marvel at marram shadow patterns.

On my walk with mantras
my heart has opened
and I feel the pain inside.
I allow it just to be,
because it is my truth.
I accept my sadness
as a gift.

I remember feeling like a tree,
and wonder now can I be grass?
Growing in the dunes,
bending with every whim of wind;
but strong and deep.
I feel a waiting for something
that may not happen for a long time,
and the patience that goes with that.

Nourished by crystal sand,
close in around me like a heavy cloak.
I see darkness and light at the same time.
I accept them both as I accept both parts in myself,
not wrong or right, but a way of being.

I am rooted, earthy and secretive
but I am also a dancer;
the wind and spray my partners.
I am slender with graceful limbs,
I never tire.

At times I do stand still
simply to be.
Sensing the beauty and the wonder around me,
and the song of the sea- the mantra of my life.

I am at one with the Dunes and the whole world.
I do not see myself as an individual plant,
our roots all intertwine.
I can't tell where one starts or ends...

Finding the Heart Space

Forgotten moments linger still
in the place that is Sanctuary,
That is the heart.

There I will fly when I need to rest,
when I need to find my peace of mind.
A chamber that is warm and safe
with a glowing light of hope.
Where I can feel the eternal stillness;
where time stops and I am free to be.
To be myself. To be free.

Everyday without fail
I need this time to be,
to become more fully me.
Because when I feel that peace inside,
I can truly flow like water,
resisting nothing, taking rocks
and boulders on my way.
Easily, freely flowing
into the awaiting adventures of my life.

Fear is left behind upstream,
no longer my travelling companion.
I choose instead the playful wind,
the life-giving sun,
the miraculous moon.

En route I meet such beautiful souls
that touch my heart
and bring tears of gratitude to my eyes,
that I was able to pass their way.

And when our streams merge,
we start the dance of synergy.
And so the flow increases
and we are all energised and renewed.
And the freer we flow,
the more intricate our dance becomes
and the more we trust that it is innate.

And as we dance we use our voices
to open our hearts even more.
Like the nightingale we sing,
pouring out our souls for all to see;
each note a mystery to be solved or resolved.

Trusting it will come out right.
Flowing with our sound,
deftly weaving magic into our lives.
Getting to the bridge
And jumping off with joy and hope in our hearts-
we are always saved,

because fear is an illusion anyway.
So we sing and give thanks
And the dance goes on.

Fulmar on the Beach

That week a close childhood friend had nearly died and we didn't know if she was going to make it. Col's Uncle Shaun had just died as well. I went for a walk and had an intense experience.
At the far end of Long Strand beach, I found a washed up Fulmar which at first glance appeared to be dead. He opened and closed his bill when he saw me but could not move. I picked him up and carried him as there were dogs on the beach. As I walked I gave him reiki. At first he seemed very ill at ease and held his head out at an awkward angle. After a few minutes I saw him looking up at me with those clear black eyes. Now he looked different. He had surrendered. He could feel my warmth and the energy and he relaxed his head into normal position. Another few minutes later, I saw his eyes had closed and knew he had died. I love these birds that have accompanied me so many times on my watches at sea. This is the first time I held one. He has that lovely musky petrel smell. I feel his energy around me, feel the place on my chest where I held him when walking. I am glad I was able to be there with him and keep the dogs away. I am saddened and yet enriched.
I sat in the Dunes and started writing.

Sometimes we are caught up in the storm of our lives.
We become helpless and are swept along with currents,
at some stage end up washed up on the beach.
There we lie, barely conscious, unable to move
or do anything to help ourselves.
It is only then, we may find the point of surrender.

On the one hand defeated, but on the other,
we finally decide to flow with life.
If death is calling us, we will go that way too.

Although physically and emotionally spent,
For the first time maybe, there is a space,
a breath, an allowing of what is.
We are finished fighting, struggling, resisting.
Now ironically at our lowest point,
we are flowing with life.
We gain clarity of what's important,
what it is we really wanted all along.
What if we could do this without going
to the brink of our lives?
What would life be like then?

The Heart of Love

Glendree, 10 June 2014

I wrote this while on an 'Earthsong Retreat' in Co. Clare after I had been re-birthed in the sweat lodge.

Sometimes surely the heart
must crack open wide.
For Love finds it's way into the fissures,
then strikes us with a moulten light
and sears us.

It leaves a permanent mark.
And it must be so,
because there is nothing
more urgent or important than Love.

Yes it is 'a many splendoured thing'.
Sometimes it hurts so much, yet
we must obey the call of Love.
Feel it in our blood, pulsing.
Reminding us of who we are
and where we've come from.
Even why we are here.

And yet sometimes the ways
of Love are mysterious to us.
We become frightened
and lose our path.
Fear becomes our new master
and we follow its orders,
gradually forgetting about Love.

But only for a while;
for we cannot ignore
our true nature forever.
The light within-
it will shine given half a chance.
It is always there flickering,
waiting to ignite.
ready to create a forest fire of the soul.
To wake us up to ourselves.

To re-realise,
that there is Love,
and we were Love
all along.

Baby Mine

*Most of the time I am fine about Alan and what happened,
but on the day this song came to me, I was feeling the full extent of my grief.*

Oh little baby, oh baby mine.
Oh little baby, where are you now?

Oh little baby, where are you now?
Oh little baby, where are you now?
Where are you now?

Oh a heart that was waiting,
waiting for a new life,
to cheer our loved ones.

I felt you in my belly,
kicking; dancing around
when we played 'Suavemente.'

I felt the love of a mother,
I didn't know I had inside of me.
You made me feel different.
I felt so happy and proud
that you came to me.

But then the day came
when you had to leave,
earlier than I wanted you to.
But I could not ask
for a different way,
'cos I knew that you,
that you couldn't stay.
That you had to go,
that you had to go,
away from me.
Oh I miss you.
Oh I miss you.

But then I hear you say,
"I never left you.

I'd never leave you
when you needed me.
Because I'm always here,

you just have to look to your heart
and feel me

'cos I'm still here.
I am here for you,
I love you too,
mother mine.
But don't worry,
everything is, as it should,
as it should be.
And we have our love for eternity
yes you and me
you and me, you and me,
you and me, you and me.

Yes you and me
have had lifetimes
of adventures in the past,
and we know each other so well.
We are always one together,
helping each other
on our way,
on our way.
Gifts on our way".

Baby where are you now?
My baby where are you now?
Not in the clouds, I know that.
I know that,
'cos I feel you around.
Feel you around me,

loving me, protecting me,
guiding me.

Oh baby mine, I miss you, I love you.
Oh baby mine, I miss you, I love you.

Thank you for what you've given to me;
the gift of a mother.
Thanks to you,
I now have two little boys,
happy and healthy and kind.
Growing taller than their little brother in heaven,
their brother in heaven, their brother in heaven.
Oh baby mine, oh baby mine,
Oh baby mine, brother in heaven.
Oh baby mine, oh baby mine,
Oh baby mine, oh baby mine.

I love you, oh baby mine, forever.
Oh baby mine, stay with me.
Oh baby mine, for ever
Oh baby mine, oh baby mine.
Oh baby mine, oh baby mine.
Oh baby mine.

On Loss and Abundance

On 1 September 2014, I committed to my book about Alan and started typing up my diary entries. This process stirred up lots of memories and I went down to the beach the next day and wrote this piece there. Two days later, I went to the Clonakilty Writer's Group in the library for the first time. I wasn't ready to read any of my diary out but I read them this poem. It was a surreal experience being in the library and publicly telling a group of strangers the background to my story and why I was there. It was the first time I mentioned Alan or angels in public. I am so appreciative of the support and friendship I have found there. I am being given the courage to be vulnerable.

I
Loss

Women in Afghanistan eat vanilla ice-cream in secret.
On the beach, I savour a chocolate chip cookie.
Women united by pleasure.

Day two of writing Alan's story and I cried
as I typed; reliving that week in hospital.
Astonishment,
     Perfection,
       Grace,
         Love,
           Heart-break,
             Loss,
               Bittersweet
                 Goodbyes.

This path of pain has brought me to who I am today.
A mother to two more fair haired boys. A woman
discovering her voice, finding herself in the place of things.

While I walked along the beach, pensive, reflective,
I could feel my angels bumping into me, trying to make me laugh.
And they did, even though I didn't want them to. 'I'm being sad
at the moment' I said. 'Stop interrupting me'.

But they smiled and said 'Emotions are not exclusive. You can be sad
and happy and notice the exquisite beauty all around you.'

II
Abundance

Ephemeral art   created by   the sea
    Individual strands of seaweed pasted
        to the wet sand making patterns,
            for the sheer joy of creation.
            Already they are removed
                by the incoming tide,
        without any sense of loss.
The sea knows abundance;
        trusts in creativity.
            Why she curves
                each wave
            picture perfect
    in the moment.   The sea never worries
                        about running out of waves.
                    There is always more.
                        Trust and create,
                        create and trust
                        and trust...

51

Caramel Swirls

Dreamy caramel,
lulls me in deep.
Melted chocolate,
velvety sweet.

Stepping stones,
a rickety bridge,
leads me to something new;
or maybe something old and unseen in the shadows.

Golden sunlight ,
warms me.
Giving me comfort
I swim in the patterns,
feeling renewed.

Immersed in swirls,
Dancing light,
Reflects the colours that sooth.

Dreamy caramel,
lulls me in deep.
Melted chocolate,
velvety sweet.

Wellsprings

Today my heart is bursting with sadness. It's Alan's 9th Anniversary.
I want to stay present and feel it all. I feel something needs to be expressed.

In the quiet fall of the evening,
there is a wellspring of Love
deep at the heart of matters.
Flowing down, I listen and wait
feeling the energy pulsing within.
Surrounding me with an aura of calm
from the inside out.
I am held in Love.

Inside, the meaning of the words lies hidden,
like a crystal in a rock awaiting discovery.
The gemstones will be spilled when the time is right,
casting lighted shadows.
My face is an open window
and I feel the draught under my nose.
I am lifting layers in my head and looking under.

Sometimes I catch a glimpse
As a small crab under a rock
scuttles away when the rock is raised.
The space within the space,
the voice within the voices.
The many layers of our dimensions
waiting to be deciphered.

In between the tapestry of words
are the ones I seek.
When the words come stiltingly slow,
I know they are not my own,
but a guidance to me-
Words to be treasured.

New Beginnings

*I woke up one morning after dreaming this story of a young soul and an older
wiser soul planning a new incarnation.*

"Okay, so you get three goes, what then?"
"Well if you are not successful, you have to forfeit 50 years."

"That's not too long I suppose,
but if only one of us makes it, we'll be out of sync,
that's past middle age. What if I can't find you?"

"We will find each other, Destiny will play her part.
 Don't worry; when we get there it will all work out, you'll see.
It always does. Throughout our lives everything will
happen precisely when it's meant to according to Divine timing.

All you need to do is stay present.
 You get to experience everything, feel everything.
You will feel kind of dense. Your body forms a container for you.
It works in tandem with gravity to keep you grounded.
As usual you will have your intuition of course that is your birthright.
In addition you will have five earthly senses -
sight, touch, hearing, taste and smell.
The weird thing is, you will forget nearly everything you know now.
Even your intuition may go to sleep.
It's just part of the Earth spell.

The game is to live blindfolded so to speak from the truth
of who you really are, but always you are having experiences-
feeling pain, pleasure, sorrow, confusion, anger, love.
Little by little you start to wake up again and if you can remember
the ways of love and who you truly are, then you become enlightened
and can move on to the next level of the game."

"It sounds exciting and scary as well.
 I do want to give it a go though

and knowing I'll find you some day gives me hope and strength.
How will I recognise you?"

"That's easy. You'll just look in my eyes and feel pure love and oneness.
You'll feel as if you've always known me, which of course you have!
Remember young soul, I've done this before many times.
It is my mission to guide and protect you down there.
It is written in the sacred texts of soul agreements.
I will be there for you. You will also have your angelic and spirit guides
always on hand to advise and protect you.
The only difficulty is that you may not even remember
or believe they are there.

There is a system of separation on Earth, all part of the illusion.
In reality, we are all always connected to one another
but you may not be able to feel it all the time.
Your perception will be clouded during your time there.
It's just part of the game really."

"It all seems very strange and challenging,
yet I can't wait to try out my new body,
meet my parents, my brothers and sisters and feel their love.
I want to roam barefoot on the Earth Mother, meet her creatures,
taste her fruits, meet the elements.
I will scatter light as I go, in joyful celebration of the Divine.
I am ready.
Can we go yet?"

"Yes, it's time.
Remember take three deep breaths to reset and always follow your heart.
See you on the other side!"

Memorial

This dedication is to the memory of our loved ones who have passed away. We, their family and friends have put them forward to honour them and to show our enduring love. I am offering a sound healing for everyone named as well as their loved ones with the intention set for healing for all, that we may come to a place of acceptance and knowing, that Love lives on.

Today, on a 'secret side of the beach',
there is a vibration,
rising up above the surf and sand.
Hovering and floating
on the cresting waves.
Spreading out like a blanket of love.
Not for herself,
for 'Self' is absorbed
into the churning waves,
cleansing intention.

What hovers out there, is pure.
It is intention,
It is prayer,
It is for the memory
of the passing ones,
whose journey extends beyond time,
and for those who remain here,
who feel the distance,
of their loved one's journey.

So upon these waves,
is the prayer,
is the intention,
is the vibration
transcending space and time,
where a loved one's ear,
travelling the beyond,
is caught for a moment,
with a message,
with a whisper,
with an intention,
rising up from the
waters of the earth.

A message of love,
a message of memory,
and a moment suspended,
for 'Union' and 'Healing'.

Ronan Murray

"In Memory of Our Loved Ones.."

Alan,	Fearghal Murphy,	John,
Ross,	Sybil O'Kelly,	Sean,
Bradley,	Patrick,	Marie Colette,
Uncle Mal,	Rose,	Evelyn,
Don,	Christopher Ernest,	Kevin,
Catherine O'Connor,	Keith John,	Tom,
Christopher David Roy Magee,	Patricia Mary Anne,	Martha,
Barry Johnson,	Virginia Mary,	Michelle,
Robert E. Murray,	Nana & Grandad Riordan,	Niamh,
Baby P.,	Nan & Grandad Poll,	Enno,
3 Sleeping Babies,		Julia

Decade

10 January 2015

Alan's 10th Anniversary
Mum and Dad and Lou and Dave coming down today to join us. If it's not too cold we will have our usual picnic by the graveyard. Special muffins this year with white chocolate and marshmallows.

I sit at the bare pine table
struck
with the knowing
I was so lucky
No other child has shaped me so.

Ten years on
still he is here
gently guiding
me along
my chosen path
that I could not
see before him.

Song for Alan

I am aboard the FRV Scotia for a fortnight conducting seabird and cetacean surveys in the North Sea. The other night I wrote words to Alan's Song, and when I was singing it, he tickled my head when I sang 'the brush of your wings'. I felt so happy and peaceful and close to him.

At night I lie on my bed
waiting for you.
Then together we fly over,
over the waves,
over the sea of our dreams.

Loneliness
brings me closer to you,
at last in heaven.
Feel the brush of your wings
in starlight,
at last in heaven.

Fireside pictures
come to mind,
sparks of light renew,
There was never a doubt
of my love for you,
at last in heaven.

You were my firstborn
whom I longed to hold,
hold you in my arms.
Hold you forever,
hold you in my arms,
but then you left me.
Said you had to go.

Now loneliness
brings me closer to you,
at last in heaven.

Feel the brush of your wings
in starlight,
at last in heaven.

It seems that sadness
brings me closer to you.
I won't let go,
won't let go
oh I love you so.

Feel the brush of your wings
in starlight.
At last in heaven.
At last in Heaven.
At last in Heaven.

Interview with Alan under the Apple Tree

I wrote this after meditating on my wooden chair under my favourite apple tree.
The questions, I wrote with my right hand and the answers with my left.

Why did you have to leave so soon?
We are a soul family and we decided this together.
Everything happened in Divine Order.

What does that mean?
There is a time and a place for everything.
In spirit linear time does not exist.
My time on Earth was short and sweet. I felt your love and I feel it now.
I was spiritually nurtured in your loving care
and I did not feel any physical pain.
I did not suffer.

Where are you now?
I am home. I am the one-ness.
It's more a state of being
than an actual place.

Are you happy?
Of course. I am the light.
I am the moon and stars. I am at one.

What was your purpose in life?
A tree grows many roots that spread far underground.
There are many interconnected reasons.
How do you describe the ripple caused by a stone
thrown in the water?
Each concentric wave looks separate but is connected
to the one before it.

What should we do when someone we love dies?
We must always accept what is. Stay in the present.
Be in the moment. Feel your emotions.
They will guide you.
Have compassion for yourself and others.
Remember love is not bound by time and space.
Love is always the answer.

Dream Sequence

As a busy mother, most of my writing is done early morning between wake and sleep. Sometimes I get glimpses..

I Aurora
11 Feb 2015

In the half-light
there is time
to be
in sleepy wakefulness
pondering life's
meaning
through scattered dreams.

Bridging chords
that help with endings
or bring you back
to the start
for a second chance.

My head unfurls
its thoughts and concerns
empties on the page
leaving me lighter
setting me up
for the day
in a way
I did not know before.

I remember now
I was on a ship
hurtling through space.
The highlight
sitting on a beanbag
in the dark,
watching the live mass.

All those beautiful stars
and then Northern lights
red and green
lighting up the room.

II The Morning Channel
27 Feb 2015

Is the morning the time to channel
I wonder?
When long icecream stares
suspend time.
if I don't blink much

and keep my gaze out of focus
I can still retrieve
my disentangled dreams.
On the inside
the wakeful thoughtful
bit of me is there too,
just not as bossy as usual.

Every morning as I write
I hear the sea,
loud and constant,
reminder
of this place
where I have rooted.

I feel the cat beside me
solid purring black and warm,
although she's not actually here.
Stirrings upstairs;
soon my little world
will expand
with noisy chatter and laughter.

III Ode to Mornings
4 Mar 2015

If I stay muted,
I can stay in the zone.
Gentle energy
swirling through my head.
Dreaming thoughts and pen combine,
keeps me from joining the waking
world.

My kids discuss the rules
of hexbug rugby.
I am apart.
I am inside.
Observing.
Unaffected,
as when heavy rain
bangs on the window
and we are snug inside.

If I were a snail,
I would be half
out of my shell,
antennae concealed.
Motionless
waiting
sensing
all that is
from a dreamlike
perspective.

It turns argumentative.
Voices raised,
with insistent, intensity.
Calls me back
like Keat's bell,
extricating him
from the nightingale's
enchantment.
'Fled is that vision,
do I wake or sleep?'

IV Dreamtime
2 Apr 2015

There is this
strip of land
on the horizon
and a blue-green sea
in-between.

I can just about
taste the feeling
but its meaning
is forgotten.

Alan is applying himself
to be a limpet
and he is successful.
Now I see him in a shroud
small and serious.

Everything is not as it seems
Those freckles cannot be
and yet they are his,
in dream and in truth.

Thumping feet upstairs,
a hairdryer.
Outside, light
pours through daffodils.
Between sleep and waking,
I search the tideline
for these small treasures.

Letting Go

I'm asking for just one word today... LOVE
Thank-you. That's what this book is all about really. It's about reassurance that our love is safe even in death. That even though we feel alone and separate, it is not true. We are LOVE and we are so very LOVED. We have angels and spirit guides with us all the time encouraging us gently and are always there if we ask for guidance. We are not apart from our loved ones who have passed either. In the early days and weeks after Alan's passing, I was aware of a ball of energy to the right side above my head. It took me a while to realise it was Alan because I was not used to feeling the presence of spirit. Now every Friday, when I go shopping in the market, he finds me a parking space usually with unerring timing. A car will drive out and I can drive straight in. It doesn't matter if it's a very busy time or there are 5 other cars in front of me, I will get a space. My inward journey of growing up spiritually and emotionally has all been guided by Alan. This is still work in progress and always will be. On Saturday I went for a healing session with Pina Lazara, a local spirit medium and had a wonderful session. She saw my 'fair-haired' firstborn and said he was helping me with the healing. I read her memoir and loved it. In her book, Pina admits she was reluctant to write the book because she was afraid people would think she was crazy. But she did write the book and overcame her fear of what other people think. This is a big thing for me too. I am just learning how to be comfortable in my own skin, completely being myself, not relying on approval from others.

Inside my heart there is an ocean.
I can hear the roaring of the waves.
I want to sing that song,
bathe in the cool waters.
Immerse myself in the currents
flow
towards
adventure
wonder and delight.

Usually I wonder how
I can get there.
I shrug and act helpless
as if my mind ran the show.
But today is different.
I can go there
easily,
simply
by letting go.

Sometime Soon

Sometimes when I'm at home a song will come to me and I just record it quickly before it's gone. The boys were playing noisily in the background as I sang it.

You'll be coming round again soon,
coming round again soon,
coming round again soon.

Since that day when you were a football sized bump
I was so happy just being your mum,
I was just happy carrying you in my tum.
I was so happy thinking what life was gonna be…

Things don't always turn out the way we think they will.
Sometimes things don't turn out the way
we expect them to.

chorus
Sometime soon you will be coming around.
Sometime soon you will be coming around.
Sometime soon you will be coming around,
and when you do,
I will be waiting for you.
I will be waiting for you.

The years pass quickly.
Things have changed around here now.
Two boys laughing and playing,
laughing and playing.

But in the corner of the room,
we have pictures of you.
Pictures of you in my arms brand new.
You would be 11 by now;
11 by now.

chorus

Camino

2013 was a big year for me spiritually. I decided to follow my dreams of writing. I went away with my sister Lou for a week to walk the end of the Camino from Santiago de Compostela to Finisterre. It was the longest I had been away from my kids since they were born.
During the walk there was time to think and my bittersweet sadness would surface.

Oh what would be a fitting song for the Camino?
Would it be full of cramping calves and tired blistered feet?
Or the sense of peace and presence
in St. James' Cathedral in Santiago de Compostela?
Shocking pink flowers in a well tended garden.
A cheerful old lady gardening with her cat and dog,
happy to chat with a couple of peregrinos.

Or is it the instant camaraderie in a roadside café?
Bonded by scallop shells and a common goal.
Singing 'whisky in the jar' with the german lads;
two ukuleles, kindred spirits.
Two curious jays eyeing up the Irlandesas
with colourful bags and fresh faces.
Or maybe the unexpected greenery like home from home?

Chorus
   Aches and pains, feet, neck and calves
   are the order of the day,
   when you're on the camino.
   Face tingling from being outside,
   now in the joy of lying flat in a comfy bed.

Paddling in cool waters by a medieval bridge,
relieving stinging feet; a welcome albergué.
Playing music with Antonio, Lola the grey cat
widens her eyes in surprise.

Dinner with new friends, share tales of the camino.
United in our enthusiasm for this opportunity
to take time out to walk and reflect on our lives.

An after dinner rose for the ladies seals the night
with a delicate scent. The beauty and perfection
of her petals, hued in pink and yellow and peach.

Chorus

On a simple altar outside the hermitage
of Nuestra Senòra de Nieges. A photo
of a smiling boy called Gus,
placed by his loving mother.
Missing him, yet knowing he is happy now.
And the soft mist and rain and the heather,
reminds me of home.

Chorus

Words of wisdom from Lou.
'Hydrate when you're static.
The camino is all about your legs!'

It's all over now; our camino.
Over now; our camino.
Buen camino!

Tell Mama

Last night Cian Finn and Anne-Marie Hynes played an amazing candlelit acoustic gig in Clonakilty. This morning I woke up with the first line of a reggae song in my head… My mum had a couple of miscarriages and I felt it was a message from my brother who wanted to let us know everything was okay. His message was one of love and I felt the strength of our sibling bond.

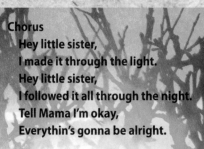

Chorus
   Hey little sister,
   I made it through the light.
   Hey little sister,
   I followed it all through the night.
   Tell Mama I'm okay,
   Everythin's gonna be alright.

As soon as I went,
the angels they come to me.
They smiled and they joked,
they said 'Hey long time no see'.

Chorus

So Mama don't you worry,
I'm just fine honestly.
I followed the light,
I'm alright.
See you in eternity.

Thank-you for this chance to Be,
Just here for a little while.
Thank-you for your love and protection,
now you've set me free.

Chorus

Tell Mama I'm okay,
I'm all love and light.

Grandmother

This piece about my late mother-in-law was inspired after hearing a poem at the 'Psoken Wrod' the night before when Alison Ducker paid a lovely tribute to her father. My sister-in-law Alayne was visiting at the time from the Isle of Lewis and she always reminds me of Ross.

She brought shells from the island,
placed them on your grave.
Made me re-baked potatoes
when I was carrying Cillian.

Ross, deep and wise as a peaty pool
slowly stirred.
You did not gush.
You did not believe in angels but
you saw the orb circle three times
round the telegraph pole in your garden.
Long enough to confirm your puzzlement
and know you had not imagined it.
Your slow cook love simmered,
infusing all of us.
At your funeral we flew paper darts
with messages and drawings of love
into your grave.

The loneliness when you were gone.
The signs you sent to say you were still here,
The Wiggle's guitar playing random tunes on it's own;
the flapping solar penguin jumping off the window sill.
Your treasury of paintings, prints and quilts.
Your modesty
that had not shown them to us before.

The night I dreamt of you in India,
warm balmy night,
four poster bed with swaying muslin sides.
You wore white linen and a golden tan.
You looked at me with your blue McClean eyes;
smiling beatifically.
Told me you were fine.

Leanbh na spéire

I was on watch one day at sea, when this lament came to me as Gaeilge.

Tá mo leanbh, tá mo leanbh,
tá mo leanbh, 'na chónaí sa spéir.
Tá mo leanbh, tá mo leanbh,
tá mo leanbh, 'na chónaí sa spéir.

Ó leanbh, ó leanbh,
ó leanbh, an bhfuil tú ann?
Ó leanbh, ó leanbh,
ó leanbh, an bhfuil tú ann?

Aréir bhí na réalta, aréir bhí na réalta,
aréir bhí na réalta ag lasadh an spéir.
Aréir bhí na réalta, aréir bhí na réalta,
aréir bhí na réalta ag lasadh an spéir.

Ó máthair ghealaigh, ó máthair ghealaigh,
ó máthair ghealaigh, tabhair aire don pháiste dom.
Ó máthair ghealaigh, ó máthair ghealaigh,
ó máthair ghealaigh, tabhair aire don pháiste dom.

Caoiním mo pháiste, caoiním mo pháiste,
ach san oiche réaltach, tuigim 'bhfuil sé sásta.
Caoiním mo pháiste, caoiním mo pháiste,
ach san oiche réaltach, tá sé sásta.

Tuigim a mhúirnín, tuigim a stórín,
go bhfuil tú sásta i measc réalta na spéire.
Tuigim a mhúirnín, tuigim a stórín,
go bhfuil tú sásta mar réalta sa spéir.

Mo ghrá thú a linbh, mo ghrá thú a linbh,
mo ghrá thú a linbh, mar réalt 'san spéir.
Mo ghrá thú a linbh, mo ghrá thú a linbh,
Is tusa mo leanbh, mo leanbh na spéire

Child of the Sky

Translation from the Gaeilge.

My child, my child,
my child is living in the sky.
My child, my child,
my child is living in the sky.

Oh child, oh child,
oh child, are you there?
Oh child, oh child,
oh child, are you there?

Last night the stars, last night the stars,
last night the stars were lighting the sky.
Last night the stars, last night the stars,
last night the stars were lighting the sky.

Oh mother moon, oh mother moon,
oh mother moon, mind the child for me.
Oh mother moon, oh mother moon,
oh mother moon, mind the child for me.

I cry for my child, I cry for my child,
but in the starry night I know he is happy.
I cry for my child, I cry for my child,
but in the starry night, he is happy.

I know darling, I know love,
that you are happy among the stars of the sky.
I know darling, I know love,
that you are happy as the stars of the sky.

My love be with you child, my love be with you child.
My love be with you, child who is like a star in the sky.
My love be with you child, my love be with you child.
You are my child, my child of the sky.

Connections

John Riordan

I have had incredible help and support in collating this book. Two of my friends, John and Jonathan have written poems in response to hearing Alan's story. I was very moved but the best bit was that I felt another person outside my immediate family had been touched by Alan. I am delighted, they have given me permission to include them here.

Last night searching for the Northern Lights
I thought you might be looking up at the same sky
for the bright star Realta, where your son abides.

You who sang acapella in the stillness of the library
or played your ukulele through the noise of Bantry Market,
busking your heart out like Laurie Lee
walking through Spain "one midsummer morn".

Cool, compereing the Spoken Word live mic
Happy, playing with the kids on long Strand
or tracking Harriers across mountain and moor.

His soul is free, unfettered,
watching over you like a Guardian Angel,
waiting for time to soften your grief
and let your restless spirit be.

Bestowed Upon Me
Jonathan Jennings

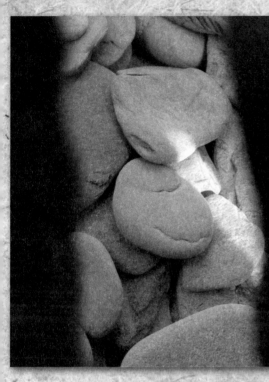

Bestowed upon me
Is a love
Burden now released
Deceased
This I say
With a tear in my eye

I smile , my son
I see your smile
The creation of my day
You paved the way
Your memory's much stronger
Much stronger than I

A satellite for all
All those who dare
Not all blessed
With a full chore, of care
Bestowed upon me
I too, have dared.

Summer

I am so blessed and grateful to have my two sons, Cillian (10) and Jamie (7) in my life.
This song was about a perfect summer's day we shared together.

Jamie woke up this morning
snuggling, looking for his brekkie,
the bed was oh so comfy.
Cillian was there too for his cuddles,
I'm feeling relaxed.

Some beautiful sage,
now I'm ready to take on the day.
It's glorious outside, sea flat calm.
Not a single cloud in the clear blue sky.

Chorus
   Oh summer, don't you just love it?
   Bright red strawberries and the promise of the beach.

We'll go down to the Long Strand
with a picnic and go
to the secret side of the beach.
The tide is in, we can play in the rock pools.
Find the shrimps and the crabs
and have a little dip.
It's so lovely to cool down
in the shimmering sparkling sea.

And later when the tide is out,
we'll go and visit the troll's cave.
Lucky for us, they're mostly not in,
but they don't seem to mind
when we borrow their spades.

Chorus

Shine

What's in my heart wants to pour out.
What it is, I don't know yet.
I feel a yearning inside,
a desire to speak my mind.
To be heard, to be understood.
The time for misinterpretation
is past, now is the time of open heart.
My emotions are freshly served,
no longer darkly brewing, under cover.
In the light there is nothing to fear.
In fact, everything is quite clear.
I can say what I mean
and mean what I say.
Such freedom is a newfound luxury.
Soon becomes a lifelong necessity.
The past is the past.
The present is my present
to me and the world.
When I shine, I can see
everyone shining too.
See their inner light.
Our shared vulnerability
is our secret strength.
I'm gonna shine,
so the whole world can see.
'Cos when I shine, I see you shine in me.
And when we shine, the whole world can see
that there is light at the end of the tunnel.
I'm gonna shine, you're gonna shine
We're gonna shine.
Shining, shining, shining, shining.
Shining, light up the world.

Shores of Yours

Paddy Pollock

Soothe the springs of our inner being,
as we imagine the shores of yours,
and wait patiently for our turn of tide,
to land with joy and there abide.

Afterword

I love to sing. For me it feels like flying, the way I do in my dreams. It brings me a feeling of weightlessness and freedom. It's a place where I can see opportunities and I can shed my own and others preconceptions of me. I am in the moment and free to choose the way I will go. Singing calms me, brings me to my centre, grounds me, fulfils me.

Writing songs and poems and taking photos are my favourite ways of being creative. Until recently I never even thought of myself as a creative person. My creativity was buried and I didn't know it was there. Now I am embracing my artistry and femininity and realising that these aspects work in tandem and allow me to flow in creative choices and expression.

When Alan died everything changed for me. What was supposed to be the worst thing that ever happened to me, turned out to be the greatest blessing. I have learnt so much from Alan- joy, pain, heart-breaking sorrow, grace, acceptance, love, compassion, empathy. But most importantly he showed me how short and precious this lifetime is and not to waste it wondering what could have been.

After working as an ecologist for over 20 years, I have been moving towards doing something new in my life- working as a holistic therapist and singer-songwriter and poet. I am currently in practice in Clonakilty offering sound healing treatments and angel card readings.

I am blessed to live in West Cork looking out at the sea, with my husband Col and our sons Cillian (10) and Jamie (7).

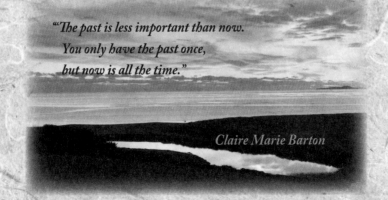

"The past is less important than now.
You only have the past once,
but now is all the time."

Claire Marie Barton

Acknowledgements

First I want to thank my husband Col who has been my rock for the past 20 years. He always has his feet planted firmly on the ground and stops me from floating off. Over the past couple of months he has cooked and cleaned  and played with the kids while I often turned into a mumble from my laptop. He has held everything together allowing me the freedom to write this book. Col, my love and gratitude always. I thank my sons Cillian and Jamie for the joy they bring me and their patience as I worked on this book.

I thank my family, my mum and Dad - Paddy and Phil, my sister Lou and my brother Dave for their love and support always. Thanks Lou and Dad for all your help with the fundraising.

Once I decided to write this book, I got so much support. I especially thank all my friends from the Clonakilty Writer's Group especially John Riordan and Nick Smith who reviewed a draft of the book, and to Moze Jacobs, Isobel Baldwin, Michael Ray, Afric McGlinchy, Ann Dineen, Brendan McCormack, Mary Rose McCarthy, Fiona Frisby, Hugh Bradley, Jack Kelleher, Sr. Laurenza Kelly, Sr. Bernadette Collins, Peter Crisson and Trace Irvine all of who critiqued many of the pieces in this book. Thanks to Sr. Bernadette and John for helping with Leanbh na Spéire. Thank you Frances Bermingham-Berrow for allowing me to share your story. Thank you Moze for taking time out to talk to me about the book project at a time when I was stuck. Thanks to Annette Skade for ideas on developing the book. Thanks to Breda Wall Ryan for reviewing the book. Thanks to all my friends at 'Psoken Wrod' who are both inspiring and very supportive.

Ronan Murray deserves huge thanks for all the work he has put into this book, both on the graphic design front to the recording of the pieces. Thank you Ronan for your patience, cheerfulness, enthusiasm and dedication to getting this book out into the world!

Thank you John Riordan, Jonathan Jennings, Ronan Murray, and Paddy Pollock for allowing their poems to be included in this book. Also thanks to George Helou for permission to use his quote from his book 'Angelic Dreams'.

My Uncle Mal died about 8 weeks ago. He was my friend and confidant and pen-pal since I was a child and he was working out in the missions in Zambia. His sight deteriorated in the last few years and I wanted to make the CD of this book especially so that he could listen to it. He never got to hear it but I dedicate the CD to his memory. He taught me so much about the value of friendship and family and fun, and all were equally important to him.

I thank Andrea Beadle who really got me going with discovering what I wanted to do with myself and prompted the writing of this book. Thanks to Rev. Elvia Roe, and all my friends at Angels Teach & Living with the Angels for all their support and the amazing angel card readings that helped to guide this book! Thanks to Christine Mitchell Marzano for the lovely angel card reading last week which kept me calm during the fundraising!

Thanks to all the mentors and healers I have worked with on my journey - Maan Kantar, Andrea Beadle, Lisa Carvill, Roz Lawlor, Pina Lazaro, Louise Pollock, Jaimi Blakely, Helen Harrington, Pamela Jordan, Jo Beth Young, Guillermo Rozenthuller, Sonia Choquette, Pam Rennie, Marilyn Harper, Wendy Hart, John Bowker, Elizabeth Ewing, Melanie O'Reilly, Rene Marie. So grateful for the wonderful Earthsong camps where tears are always welcome and I am able to be totally me and where my journey into sound healing began with Chrys Blanchard. Thank you to the College of Sound Healing for supporting me on my journey. Thanks Caz Jeffries for the song-writing workshops that got me started.

Thank you Fiona Donnelly, Fearghal, Brenda and PJ Coogan at 96Fm who helped me spread the word about my book project. Thanks to Cillian Lohan for lending me his voice recorder for the sound healing.

A Great BIG THANK YOU!
to my KickStarter Backers

I got an amazing response, and I am eternally grateful for your help in getting this book printed. I am humbled by your generosity of spirit and faith in me to deliver.

You are Andrea Beadle, Helen Arthur, Louise Pollock, Karen Kennedy, Toni Walters, Pat & Mathew Mulcair, Steve Sanders, Paddy & Phil Pollock, Nila Shah, Christine Deady, Ronan Murray, Chris Blanchard, Carol Woodford, Seana Kevany, Alice Glendinning, Sarah Leather, Julia Pallone, Celia Libera, Ciaran Cronin, Abi Brewer, Rev Elvia Nina Roe, Julie Crockett, Katja Rep, Martha O'Sullivan, Francisco Rebollo, Caz Jeffries, Moze Jacobs, Maresa Gieles, Florence Vion, Greg Bradley, Jack Kelleher, Clodagh Simonds, June Fairhead, Elaine McGoldrick, Christine Mitchell Marzano, Isobel Towse, Cillian Lohan, Teresa Wicksteed, Pam Rennie, Caroline Seyedi, Olive Walsh, Wendy Nairn, Angela Veale, Elizabeth Ewing, Sinead Fitzgerald, Dave & Colette Pollock, Carol Nichols, Nicky Rowberry, Marilien Romme, Sharon McSweeney, Samira, Martin & Parvin Branch, Dermot & Marietta O'Kelly, Charo Martinez, Janine Murphy, Diana Duggan, Fiona Ronan, Fionuala Ní Chonaill, Breda Wall Ryan, Sebastien Revon, Ita Murphy, Ronan, Sound4Healing, Linda Coyle, Pamela Marshall, Andy Webb, Louise Ross, Lucie K, Eleanor Moore, Imelda Staunton, Geoff Oliver, Kathleen O'Hara Farren, Ann, Tom & Deirdre Kearney, Loucie, Angie Cagney, Claire Cross, Lucia Sheehan, Lisa Brinkmann, Brian McSwiney, Orela Kingston, Tricia & Alan, Deirdre Ryan, Liam Collins, Emily, Gill Evans, Fr. Jim Pollock, Gena Lumbroso, Elizabeth Mee, Jonathan Jennings, Jenny O'Hare, Liz Bardyn, Maria, David Hayes, Richard Mundy, Helen, Beverlee Goynes, Julia Fox, Sally Ann Lenehan, Joyce O'Sullivan, David & Hilary Heggie, Fiona O'Shaughnessy, Rona & Will Helps, Zoe Crutchfield, Donagh Noone, Alayne Barton, Joy Pollard, Elaine O'Connell, Lily & Roy O'Sullivan, Nick Smith, Faith Wilson, Ria Lawlor, Fiona Madigan, Fiona Chance, Noelle O'Riordan, Hugh Bradley, Lisa Curran, Carmel Williams, Claudine Depreter, Marjorie Walsh, Phil Buckley, Phyllis Coughlan, Eileen Bullock, Zenaida Petre, Edel O'Donovan, Noreen Noonan, Fr. McCarthy, Olga Carpenter, Colette Barrett, Mary O'Leary, Peggy O' Sullivan,

John O'Sullivan, Eileen O'Leary, Breda Hodnett, Rosel Dabi Cullinane, Phil Guerin, Jojo Winkelmann, Marie O'Donovan, Geraldine O'Sullivan, Deirdre Hodnett, Maureen Lahiff, Christine Lahiff, Helen Gough, Magdalena Synowiec, Melissa Stanton, Joan McCarthy, Tracy McCarthy, Alison Kingston, Olive Finn & Andy Beattie, Phil Guerin, Alison Ducker, David Bateman, Phil Guerin, Sharon Calanan, Ulrike & Thomas Reidmüller, Teresa McShane, Regina O'Brien, Carol Sparling Gordon, Susan King, Caoilfhionn Casey, Roisin Hanrahan and Ian & Sharon Gordon.

Thanks to Joyce O'Sullivan and Tracy McCarthy and all the therapists from Solace Holistic Centre, Clonakilty who helped me organise a fundraiser and Sally Ann Lenihan and Charo Martinez for helping out at our coffee morning and all our friends and neighbours who came to the coffee morning and did baking. Thank-you Seana Kevany and Jonathan Coe for hosting a coffee morning to raise funds for the book.

Finally a huge thanks goes to all our family and friends- too many to name here, who supported us after Alan's death in so many ways, we will never forget your kindness. We are also very grateful to all the medical staff in both the Erinville and St. Finbarr's hospital for their wonderful care.

And last but not least I thank Alan and all my angels and guides for being with me in this adventure!

**Even through
the darkest of nights
the light does come...**

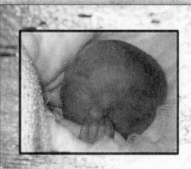

*In loving memory
of
Alan Barton*

10 January 2005

*If you feel sad
Do think of me
For that's what I'll like.
When you live in the hearts
Of those you love
Remember then...
You never die.*

*Do not stand at my grave and weep,
I am not there, I do not sleep.
I am a thousand winds that blow,
I am the diamond glints on snow.
I am the sunlight on ripened grain,
I am the gentle autumn rain.
When you awaken
in the morning's hush,
I am the swift, uplifting rush
of quiet birds in circled flight.
I am the soft stars that shine at night.
Do not stand at my grave and cry,
I am not there: I did not die.
So heed, hear when you awaken
what I say,
I live with you, I guard your way.*

**... streaming in
om the magic dawn
mbrace of the sun.**

Ronan Murray